ANGLESEY ABBEY, Cambridge

In common with many other ecclesiastical buildings in East Anglia the Augustinian Priory at Anglesey was converted to secular use in the sixteenth century and only the chapter house and vaulted monks' parlour survive. There have been several owners of the abbey, including one Hobson, a carter from nearby Cambridge, who gave to our language the expression 'Hobson's choice'. In 1926, however, Anglesey's history took a more illustrious turn when the estate was bought by Huttleston Broughton, later to become the first Lord Fairhaven. It was he who bequeathed Anglesey to the National Trust in 1966 and his nephew, the third Lord Fairhaven, now lives here.

The family was rich and when money is allied to a great and eclectic love of the arts the results can be stunning. Lord Fairhaven set about filling the rebuilt and extended Abbey with an extraordinary collection of *objets d'art*, all in pristine order and of outstanding workmanship. There is a bronze cat from Egypt, 2,500 years old; the Garter bestowed by Henry VII on Maximilian I in 1489; Thomas Gainsborough's paintbox; a whole range of clocks – all working – and in the specially built lower gallery are two of Claude Lorrain's finest paintings, dated 1663 and 1675.

Fortunate is the man who can indulge taste in this fashion, but how much more fortunate is today's traveller who can walk through Anglesey's treasure-house.

And yet even more impressive is the scale of the gardens created by Lord Fairhaven out of the flat fen surrounding the abbey. Covering 100 acres, the gardens are provide the varie can never achiev is classical statu furniture within t is over a quarter the busts of twelve Roman emperors, monumental bronze urns, and lead figures.

In spring cowslips dot the meadows and the scent of over 4,000 white and blue hyacinths fills the air. The rafts of daffodils give way to dahlias and colourful herbaceous borders, and in the autumn the varied array of trees and shrubs display every shade of red and bronze.

The old water-mill built across the 'lode' or canal that skirts the gardens is now fully restored and grinds flour from local corn at week-ends. A modern visitors' reception area provides all the creature comforts, including delicious meals at the restaurant, open from Easter until Christmas.

AUDLEY END, Essex

Owned by the nation and cared for by English Heritage, Audley End was once a Royal palace rivalling Hampton Court in size and splendour. It grew from the remains of a monastic establishment, the Abbey of Walden, which was swept away by Henry VIII, whose Speaker of Parliament, Sir Thomas Audley, was given the site by a grateful monarch.

The property duly passed to Thomas Howard, who commanded a ship in the fleet that defeated the Spanish Armada. He became the Earl of Suffolk and built a magnificent house for the vast sum of £200,000 – 'too large for a King, but might do for a Lord Treasurer', quipped James I, his jealous monarch.

Charles II, finding that the Royal palaces had suffered cruelly during the Civil War, acquired Audley End and used it for thirty-two years, but today only a few elaborate, lead rainwater heads with Royal ciphers are witness to that brief era. Samuel Pepys, the diarist, in 1677 played his flageolet in the cellars of the palace and bequeathed his superb library to Magdalene College in Cambridge, a few miles to the north.

In about 1721, following advice from John Vanbrugh, the seventh Earl pulled down most of the palace and it was not until 1765 that the then owner, Lord Howard de Walden, Baron Braybrooke, began the lengthy and very costly process of rebuilding. The care taken by the eighteenth-century craftsmen, who included Robert Adam, resulted in a building with all the appearance of a seventeenth-century mansion.

Inside there are a procession of rooms on an impressive scale and hung with family portraits. The hall boasts an elaborate wooden screen of 1605 at the north end, and an elegant one of stone at the other end. The chapel, reconstructed in 1786, is a superb example of the Georgian Gothick style and decorated in the original colours.

'Capability' Brown's sure hand is evident in the grounds of Audley End; his improvements on a grand scale are embellished by elegant garden buildings designed by Robert Adam. The circular Temple of Concord, dating from 1790, displays an inscription commemorating George III's recovery from his first attack of insanity. The magnificent early seventeenth-century stables now house an exhibition of traditional agricultural implements. There is even an Elysian garden. A plant nursery, tea-rooms, and a miniature railway help towards the complete enjoyment of a visit to this historic site.

BEESTON HALL, Norfolk

The hall presents a Gothick exterior with battlements and windows with arched tops. The walls are faced with patterned flints knapped in the East Anglia style that gives such a distinctive look to medieval buildings and churches. It is interesting that this house was designed in 1786 for Jacob Preston by William Wilkins, an architect who was responsible for such diverse buildings as the National Gallery in London and the delightful Georgian Theatre Royal at Bury St Edmunds.

Indoors the exterior style is maintained only in part; the more familiar Georgian designs are retained for the reception rooms. The door between the Gothick entrance hall and the Georgian ante-room – each side displaying its own style – is intriguing. All six rooms on the ground floor that are open to view exhibit the same excellence of proportion which is the hallmark of Georgian design.

Portraits of the Prestons adorn the walls, reminders of a family that originally bought the estate from the Hobarts of Blickling Hall and were, in turn, Royalists, Roundheads and, finally, supporters of the Glorious Revolution when James II lost his throne to William of Orange. Two were murdered by a disgruntled farm tenant over the inheritance of the Stanfield Hall estate; another was the English tax-collector at Boston, Massachusetts at the time of the 'Boston Tea Party'; several have served their county as Deputy Lord-Lieutenants and High Sheriffs. The present Baronet's father was sentenced to death by the Russian Revolutionaries for his attempts, as British Consul in Ekaterinburg, to save Tsar Nicholas II and his family from execution. Sir Thomas's work in the Diplomatic Service in Eastern Europe is commemorated by many interesting objects in the hall.

On display also is a list of duties that the late eighteenth-century servants were bidden to undertake, ranging from haymaking and clock-winding to providing a troop of cavalry. The cellars are open to show how the fine wines and spirits were stored; it is possible to buy wine as well. In the picture-gallery are displayed a constantly changing collection of works by local artists. Teas are served in the old orangery and the gardens and park are open.

For visitors who are in boats on the Norfolk Broads, the easiest access to Beeston is on foot from Neatishead Staithe, a pleasant walk of only fifteen minutes.

BLICKLING HALL, Norfolk

Lack of suitable building stone in Norfolk has resulted in great houses built of warm, red brick with stone quoins. Blickling Hall is certainly one of the finest; every person's dream of a country house, built between 1619 and 1627 in Elizabethan style with Dutch gables, corner turrets, and dominant clock tower.

One of several exceptional wooden figures on the newel posts of the staircase in the entrance hall and in wall niches above it is of Anne Boleyn, looking ill at ease in Georgian dress. Her family, as did Sir John Fastolf, Shakespeare's comic warrior, once owned the moated manor house that stood on the site of the present hall which was built by Sir Henry Hobart, James I's Lord Chief Justice. The estate eventually descended through the female line to the Lothian family and it was the eleventh Marquess of Lothian who, on his death in 1940, bequeathed the entire estate of 4,600 acres to the National Trust. He died in Washington, DC where he was British Ambassador to the USA.

The prize room in the hall is the Long Gallery, 123 feet long and unusually wide, which now houses one of the finest libraries in the country – over 12,000 leather-bound voumes, many printed before 1500. The design of the superb Jacobean

moulded plaster ceiling symbolises the Five Senses and Learning.

Several bedrooms are also open to view, one an exquisite Chinese room with hand-painted wallpaper. The walls of the Print Room are covered with engravings of paintings of great artists; these were collected in the eighteenth century just as postcards are bought today. The Peter the Great room is now restored to the magnificence of 1782 when it was created.

What draws people back to Blickling time and again are the gardens, laid out to a basic Jacobean design, colourful at all seasons and surrounded by acres of woodland. The great, square herbaceous beds glow with matching colours and beside the wide path up to the Doric Temple the azaleas and rhododendrons are all reds and yellows in early summer. The park itself, always open, has a network of footpaths and bridleways which give access to woods of ancient oak and chestnut, a pyramidal Mausoleum, a Gothick tower, and the curving lake, a mile long and full of coarse fish. The two wings of the Hall house the Regional Headquarters of the National Trust (west wing) and the restaurant, shop, and information room (east). Above the shop is perhaps the most interesting room of all, the textile conservation workshop where visitors can admire the skill of the seamstresses as they carefully repair the tapestries and furnishings of the Trust's houses in East Anglia.

In the south-east turret a lift can take disabled visitors to the first floor.

Left: The south-east corner
Above: The eleventh Marquess of Lothian
Right: The Long Gallery

BURGHLEY HOUSE, Cambridgeshire

By Queen Elizabeth I's reign country houses had ceased to be defensive and became places to be lived in and loved. Some were ostentatious and Burghley – at 240 feet by 125 feet – was definitely one of these. Completed in 1587, this grand building was owned by William Cecil, the first Lord Burghley, Treasurer to Queen Elizabeth, and the estate has belonged to the Cecil family ever since. Another dynasty of the Cecils was responsible for Hatfield House.

Inside little remains of the Elizabethan influence; the fifth Earl of Exeter who travelled widely in Europe altered the interior and had the eminent craftsmen of his day create superb Baroque ceilings, tapestries, and carved woodwork. He also filled the stately rooms with treasures collected on his tours so that today more than 700 *objets d'art* can be seen in the house.

Below: The Heaven Room
Bottom: The north front

The ninth Earl completed the task of renovation and collected yet more paintings and sculptures including the Piranesi chimney-piece in the Second George Room, of about 1765. His nephew became the first Marquess who, for his second bride, chose a beautiful peasant girl, Sarah Hoggins. Their romance was immortalised by Tennyson, himself a Lincolnshire man, in his ballad 'The Lord of Burghley'. The sixth Marquess, who died in 1981, was an Olympic hurdler, winning a Gold Medal at the 1928 Games held in Amsterdam, and also responsible for staging the 1948 Olympic Games in London.

Open to the visitor to marvel at are eighteen rooms that range from the old kitchen, the walls gleaming with burnished copper pans, to the Great Hall, over sixty feet high and used by Queen Victoria as her banqueting hall – one of many visits by royalty to this historic house. In the Pagoda Room is a formidable array of portraits, both of the family and the monarchs under whom they served.

The most flamboyant ceiling- and wall-paintings are to be seen in the Heaven Room where Antonio Verrio has created a masterful and deceptive panoply of gods and goddesses 'disporting themselves as they are wont to do . . .'. From Heaven to Hell is but a short step at Burghley for Verrio has painted the mouth of Hell overlooking the staircase that leads out of the Heaven Room.

The park is on a similar grand scale, landscaped by 'Capability' Brown and surrounded by a three-mile-long wall, built in 1796. The main entrance gates are flanked by the dramatic Bottle Lodges that date from 1801. Each year in early September three-day horse trials are held in the park.

ELTON HALL, Cambridgeshire

Here is a Gothic hall of several contrasting architectural styles, incorporating a fifteenth-century tower and a chapel equally ancient. Each elevation is very different in appearance and all is not as it seems for the battlements and turret tops were created from wood in the 1812–14 reconstruction to save expense; no doubt French prisoners of war from the nearby Norman Cross Camp were employed for the same reason.

There has been a house here since the Norman Conquest and the present owners, the Probys, have lived at Elton for over 300 years. Sir Peter Proby, who served Queen Elizabeth I in several high offices and then became the Lord Mayor of London, was granted land here. He died in 1624 and his grandson Sir Thomas, following a 'good' marriage, was able to build a mansion on this site. His account books can be seen today in the Library. In 1789 John Joshua Proby, a kinsman of William Pitt, was created Earl of Carysfort. Today William Proby, ten generations on from Sir Peter, lives in the hall and his father is Lord-Lieutenant for Cambridgeshire.

No less than eleven fine rooms are open to view. They range from the sumptuous state drawing-room in the style of a French château to a small room in the medieval tower where can be seen a bust of an old gardener who tended the gravel paths for nearly seventy years. The main library is the home of one of the finest private book collections in England – over 12,000 volumes that include rare Bibles, MSS, and even Henry VIII's prayer-book. Every room contains treasures and the family portraits are by Reynolds and Gainsborough; over the fireplace in the small dining-room is a masterpiece by John Constable of Dedham Vale.

Outside in the old stables is the family state coach used for Queen Victoria's Diamond Jubilee and in the Victorian rose-garden have been planted 1,000 roses, including many old-fashioned and highly scented varieties. Teas are served in the old billiard room. And there is even a ghost – that of Robert Sapcote whose family was at Elton before the Probys. He was inclined to rob his guests after they had left his house bearing with them their winnings after some hard gambling.

Below: The south front
Inset: The state dining-room and picture-gallery

EUSTON HALL, Suffolk

The hall is primarily about people, all royal and aristocratic, who have been portrayed by such masters as Van Dyck, Peter Lely, and Godfrey Kneller. These superb paintings hang in a series of elegant rooms in a house built by Lord Arlington, Secretary of State to Charles II. In 1671, while the King was enjoying the races on Newmarket Heath, his mistress of the moment, Louise de Kerouaille – 'that young wanton' – was staying here. Another of his good friends, Lady Castlemaine, provided him with a son, Henry Fitzroy, who was to marry Lord Arlington's only daughter, whose dowry was the Euston estates. Their son, the second Duke of Grafton, had the house remodelled but today only the north and part of the west wings remain, containing all the original rooms that survived a disastrous fire in 1900.

Lord Arlington was among the most loyal of Charles's supporters during his exile and at Euston the portraits, mostly collected by him, tell of the Royal exploits. Charles as a young prince; as a fugitive in France; Lord Arlington in his Garter robes, his nose scarred while fighting for his King during the Civil War. Up the main staircase, part of the original house of 1670, and into the square there hang more seventeenth-century portraits including that by Wissing of the rebellious Duke of Monmouth, Charles II's son by Lucy Walters, another of the King's favourites.

In the small dining-room is probably the most famous of all the pictures on display here, the charming study of mares and their foals beside the river at Euston by George Stubbs. The horses were bred by the third Duke. Also in this room is an historic view of the house and church in 1710 with a stag-hunt in progress.

The Church of St Genevieve was built on the site of a medieval church in 1676 to a design that owes much to Wren's influence. The interior, with fine plaster roofs and woodwork, remains as it was in the seventeenth century – only four other country churches of this period are known. To reach it the visitor must traverse the pleasure-grounds that display the influence of three of England's most famous landscape architects – Brown, Evelyn and Kent, whose Palladian temple boasts an octagonal banqueting room.

Teas are served in the old kitchen; and there is also a shop.

Below: The Square
Bottom: The garden front

FELBRIGG HALL, Norfolk

Remove the magnificent stands of sweet chestnut, beech and oak trees that surround Felbrigg and the North Sea would be visible; the keen winds constantly remind the visitor of the nearby coast. This corner of Norfolk was chosen by members of the great Norman family of Bigod, called de Felbrigge, for their manor and in the parish church built by them are memorial brasses and stone monuments inscribed in Norman French, a great rarity.

About 1450 the Wyndhams acquired the estate and it was a Thomas Windham who rebuilt the house in 1621–24 and also adopted the Norfolk spelling of his name. The Jacobean front, designed by the master architect Lyminge who was also responsible for Blickling Hall only eleven miles away, remains unaltered but added to it are extensions that make Felbrigg a veritable history book in brick and stone.

The west wing, completed in 1686, is in direct contrast; classical in design with a hipped roof and built of warm red bricks most probably made on the estate. Only twenty years later the orangery near by was erected for the princely sum of £261 to house during the winter the orange and lemon trees that would have dotted the formal parterre gardens round the hall.

The east wing, that joins the stables and courtyard to the original Jacobean house, was the work of James Paine in about 1751. He was also responsible for redesigning the interior of Samwell's west wing, creating the elegant dining-room, staircase, library, and the cabinet where the owner's choicest treasures were only shown to his closest friends. The plaster ceilings in these state rooms are of great merit. William Windham II went on the Grand Tour, accompanied by his tutor Benjamin Stillingfleet who later became the darling of London salons and whose blue stockings were to become symbols of learned discourse. The marvellous full-length portraits hang on the upper landing. Windham's superb collection of classical Italian landscape gouaches by Busiri still hang where he arranged them on the walls of the cabinet.

Upstairs there is a range of bedrooms which, despite their elegance and fine furnishings, appear comfortable and welcoming. The library in Gothic style contains a collection of books that reflect the scholarly taste and wide-ranging interests of the eighteenth-century Windhams. In the adjacent book-room the visitor can rest and browse among copies of old plans and documents about Felbrigg's history. The last owner, Robert Ketton-Cremer on whose death in 1969 Felbrigg was bequeathed to the National Trust, loved donkeys and so two are always to be seen in the paddock *en route* to the walled garden. The dovecot, once a home for 2,000 white doves, dominates the garden which is now restored and replanted to a traditional Georgian design.

The woodland and park are always open and two waymarked footpaths are described by guide leaflets available at the Hall.

Below: The Jacobean and Caroline fronts
Inset: The dovecot in the walled garden

GAINSBOROUGH'S HOUSE, *Suffolk*

Also described as a museum this birthplace of the famous English painter is one of the very few historic houses open throughout the year in East Anglia. Set in the centre of Sudbury it presents a classic Georgian façade which masks a complex pattern of rooms that span five centuries of gradual change. A door into the entrance hall is dated to about 1470. The garden front is quite different with two large rectangular weaving windows, a legacy of the business of weaving woollen shrouds that occupied Gainsborough's father. The family sold the house in 1792, described in the particulars of sale as a 'most excellent brick mansion . . . with two weaving shops in the Silk line, 147 ft long.'

In 1958 the house was purchased by a charitable trust and opened as an art centre and memorial to Thomas Gainsborough (1727–88). Already it can boast a fine collection of the artist's portraits on permanent loan from various other collections; and temporary exhibitions of these works are held throughout the year.

On display are some impressive works by the painter acquired by the trust, and they include what is probably the earliest extant portrait, that of a young boy. Recent cleaning by the Hamilton Kerr Institution in Cambridge has revealed part of a young girl's figure, doubtless a sister, and the quality of the brushwork and glowing colours declare vividly Gainsborough's mastery of the medium of painting.

There are several paintings by Gainsborough's contemporaries, including two works by John Constable who venerated him both as a fellow Suffolk artist and as a founder of British landscape-painting.

Several letters in Gainsborough's hand are kept at the house and in them he continually expressed his preference for landscape-painting. He painted portraits 'for the money' which, in 1750, would have amounted to only fifteen guineas for a half-length study!

Below: The garden front
Inset: Thomas Gainsborough's portrait of Abel Moysey (1743–1831)

GLEMHAM HALL, Suffolk

Motorists who speed past this country mansion should not be put off by the plain entrance front, as behind this austere façade is a comfortable dwelling, still very much home for the Cobbold family.

The building dates from the Elizabethan period although the de Glemhams owned land here as early as 1228. They did not sell the estate until 1709 and the purchaser was Dudley North whose wife, Catherine, was a daughter of Elihu Yale, founder of the American university – yet another of the strong ties that East Anglia has with the USA. Many of the treasures now on view at Glemham were gifts from Yale.

By 1722 the interior of the hall had been converted into a superb set of Georgian rooms which the visitor sees today, full of fine furniture to designs by Sheraton, Chippendale, and Hepplewhite. There are many exquisite lacquered pieces, a legacy of close ties with the East India Company.

Chinoiserie became very fashionable among the English aristocracy which explains why so much furniture with an Oriental character is found in houses like Glemham.

The imposing staircase dates from 1720 as does most of the panelling which, in the hall, has been stripped. The fine walnut furniture of the Queen Anne period is framed by four Corinthian columns.

Time must be kept to explore the beautiful rose-garden, enclosed within sheltering walls, which offers a summer-house, lily-pond, classical urns as well as traditional English symmetry. The wide lawns are framed by avenues of Irish yews; spreading cedars and beeches complete a very traditional setting for the hall.

The fifteenth-century tower of St Andrew's Church overlooks the garden and on the church walls brasses commemorate the Glemham family. The Norths are buried within the crypt beneath and there is a statue of Dudley North, a famous man of his day who was a mourner at the funeral of Sir Joshua Reynolds and a pall-bearer at the funeral of Edmund Burke.

In Glemham's cellar delicious home-made teas are served.

HELMINGHAM HALL GARDENS, Suffolk

The visitor to Suffolk may not readily equate the famous Tolly ales with the Tollemache family which, in 1886, founded the brewery of that name in Ipswich. The present Lord Tollemache lives in this moated, Elizabethan mansion built by his ancestor in 1510 and whose walls of red tile and brick provide a timeless setting for the gardens. It is not open to the public and indeed the drawbridges are raised every night to deter any intending invaders.

The 375-acre park has red and fallow deer, and rare breeds of cattle and sheep which include the agile goat-like soay whose normal diet is seaweed on its native Hebridean isles. The deer have been there as long as the massive oaks; some say for not less than 600 years and both animals and trees can be admired from the comfort of a tractor-drawn safari ride through the park. The approach to the gardens is across a smaller, Saxon moat and there, surrounded by wide lawns with two ancient black mulberry trees, are the geometric designs of a parterre garden, blue with perennial violas and scented by low, clipped box hedges.

Past walls, built in 1745, and entrance piers topped by horses' heads, the Tollemache coat of arms, and pairs of stone eagles, there opens out a traditional kitchen garden whose four square beds in Tudor style are full of vegetables in serried rows – like the Coldstream guardsmen whom generations of Tollemaches have been wont to command. Fan-trained fruit trees decorate the walls and in front of them are herbaceous plants, and old English roses rambling over iron-hooped arches.

Outside the walled gardens are the Yew, Apple and Shrubbery Walks, and a wild meadow garden covered with flowering bulbs and orchids in season. Everywhere an unending succession of colour and orderly presentation.

This is also John Constable country as the famous artist once lived in Helmingham Rectory and painted a number of versions of *A Dell in Helmingham Park* – which included an oak tree that can be seen and enjoyed today.

HINCHINBROOKE HOUSE, Cambridgeshire

This rambling Tudor house with various conversions and additions has never been entirely rebuilt despite a disastrous fire in 1830. It constitutes a remarkable story-book of architectural design which spans the centuries from Norman to modern times. It remains also as a centre of a thriving community which today uses the historic house as the VIth Form Centre of Hinchinbrooke School in Huntingdon. One of the unusual pleasures here is to be shown round by well-informed and lively pupils – who can also produce an excellent tea.

In the early thirteenth century nuns of the Benedictine Order established a priory on the site of a Norman church; stone coffins of nuns have been unearthed at various points. Life here must have been peaceful until a day in 1535 when Thomas Cromwell's Commissioner arrived to close the priory on the orders of the King. Ironically enough it was Cromwell's nephew, Richard, who was given the estate and promptly set about transforming it into a three-storey mansion. A fireplace dating from this time complete with his initials, Tudor roses, and leopards is in one of the rooms shown to visitors. His son Sir Henry continued the building of a house worthy of an Elizabethan gentleman. An imposing entrance gateway was removed from the gatehouse of Ramsey Abbey, also a Cromwellian acquisition at the Dissolution, and re-erected to the north-east of his house where it still stands. (The remains of the Ramsey gatehouse are now in the care of the National Trust.)

Two monarchs were soon to pass through this gateway, Queen Elizabeth in 1564 and, in 1603, James I on his triumphant passage down the Great North Road from Edinburgh to claim the throne of Britain. Sir Oliver was then the ambitious and extravagant owner whose lavish hospitality shown to his monarch forced an eventual sale of Hinchinbrooke to Henry Montagu, Earl of Manchester who, in turn, passed it on to his brother Sydney. It was the nephew of old Sir Oliver who became the Lord Protector and it is not surprising, therefore, that a museum is found today in Huntingdon dedicated to Cromwellian memorabilia.

Sydney Montagu's only surviving son, Edward, became one of Oliver Cromwell's trusted officers, fought at Marston Moor, and was most probably in charge of the troops that escorted Charles I on his first night of captivity – to Hinchinbrooke House! Edward's mother was a Pepys and her great-nephew became the famous diarist and also his secretary. We, therefore, have graphic accounts of Pepys's visits to his employer's mansion and of the building works that were not complete until about 1665.

Edward's grandson achieved fame by giving the name 'sandwich' to the English language – he was the fourth Earl of Sandwich and Viscount Hinchinbrooke – and by inspiring Captain Cook to embark on his voyages of exploration in the South Seas.

The Earls of Hinchinbrooke continued to serve their country well, improve their house when necessary, and it was the tenth Earl who finally renounced his title and sold the estate to the County Council in 1962.

The gardens with seventeenth-century terrace, towering cedars, and a charming rose-garden are a pleasure to walk round; the walls of the old kitchen garden now screen all the buildings demanded by a modern, thriving school.

HOLKHAM HALL, Norfolk

At the tender age of ten Thomas Coke (1697–1759) inherited his fortune and in 1712 he set off on a Grand Tour of Europe which lasted for nearly six years. His natural appreciation of classical art was reinforced by his making the close acquaintances of William Kent (whose work is so much of Houghton's glory) and of Kent's patron, Lord Burlington, whose enthusiasm for Roman architecture set an Italianate stamp on English buildings of his day. This trio's collaboration produced Holkham Hall, arguably the most beautifully balanced and monumental of all English houses with a pagan quality all its own. The exterior of sand-coloured brick, made on the estate, is slightly daunting but, once through the entrance door, the first sight of the Marble Hall is one of the great experiences of visiting country houses. Here is a room that makes a grandee of every visitor, who must then climb the splendid staircase to the next floor; a floor dedicated solely to entertainment and the display of works of art.

Thomas Coke's passion for classical art is immediately apparent from the prominence given to statuary. To this age's taste it may seem eccentric to devote one side of this vast building to the display of Greek and Roman sculpture. But the Statue Gallery reflects eighteenth-century taste at its purest, the chilly marble tempered by the warmth of William Kent's furniture placed round the walls.

The rooms that follow are all exuberant colours; the luxuriant crimson-velvet wall hangings set off to perfection the fabulous paintings in ornate gilt frames. At the head of the grand staircase is the main reception room, the saloon. The complex, patterned and heavily gilded ceiling rises thirty-two feet, occupying the attic storey above. The walls are hung in Genoese velvet. Over one fireplace hangs a portrait by Gainsborough of Thomas William Coke, known as 'Coke of Norfolk', whose crop rotations and introduction of improved breeds of sheep and cattle transformed British agriculture. The estate today covers over 25,000 acres and sound, progressive farming practice remains the hallmark of Holkham's management.

The tour of this great house includes two state bedrooms and a state sitting-room, notable for their exceptional Brussels and Mortlake tapestries, and the old kitchen with serried rows of gleaming copper and pewter vessels.

The importance of the Hall must not overshadow the scale of the Park's landscaping. In 1729 the wild land here was fenced, avenues of ilex and beech planted, and 'Capability' Brown created the lake in 1762. Humphry Repton, who once lived near Felbrigg to the east then followed and produced one of his famous Red Books for the Park, which today boasts not only an eighty-foot obelisk and a Monument to 'Coke of Norfolk', but a temple, an ice-house, and a model farm.

One of the most reliable plant nurseries in Norfolk is in the old walled garden and an exhibition of over 4,000 items of bygone times is housed in the stable block.

Below: The south front
Right: The Marble Hall

HOUGHTON HALL, Norfolk

Regarded by many as Norfolk's most memorable house, Houghton also ranks as one of England's finest. The gorgeous plumage of the peacocks that strut upon the wide lawns is colourless compared to the riches within the Hall; riches that have drawn visitors here to stare and wonder since the house neared completion in 1735. Lord Hervey came here from Ickworth and observed that the ground floor or 'rustic storey' was devoted to 'hunters, hospitality, noise, dirt and business', while the first floor – the piano nobile – was the level of 'taste, expense, state and parade'. He could have added that the attic storey housed the guests' bedrooms while the servants' rooms were in the garrets.

Sir Robert Walpole, Prime Minister in all but name to the first two royal Georges, wanted a grand house that would not only be a family residence but also permit the entertainment of royalty, aristocracy, and foreign dignitaries in as lavish and impressive a way as possible. The fashion of the time held that there should be a state apartment, a suite of rooms whose focus was the state bed. After 250 years the importance of this item of furniture has been largely lost. There are very few references to its use although it is known that the Duke of Lorraine slept in the needlework bed at Houghton in 1731. Sir Robert Walpole spent £1,200 in 1732 on gold lace for the green velvet state bed, so it was clearly for use by persons who were either very grand or thought themselves so.

At first the house may seem an alien in the Norfolk landscape, built as it is in an Italian style and in sandstone, brought by sea from Whitby to Wells. But it is given vivacity and excitement by its zestful furniture and decoration, the work of William Kent whose position in the design team was superior to that of the architect Colen Campbell. Kent's furniture both here and at Holkham Hall can be considered to be among the finest works of English art.

The varied and contrasting effects of each room are stunning and what will stay in the mind long after a visit is over are the combination of richly tinted Brussels tapestry with the needlework bed; the gilding on mahogany throughout the house; the rare English tapestry made at Mortlake depicting the factory's patron, King Charles I, and his consort; the awe-inspiring cubic Stone Hall; the contrasting delicacy of the White Drawing Room and the extraordinarily rich ceilings everywhere. Nor should the significance of the outside double stair on the west front be missed. Although part of the original design, intended to elevate the important guest immediately to the 'floor of parade', this stair was subsequently removed. It was reconstructed in 1973 by the Dowager Marchioness of Cholmondeley whose skilful and loving care for this great house is everywhere apparent. For the young-at-heart there is a collection of over 20,000 model soldiers to be admired; and real heavy horses and ponies in the stable block.

The formal layout of the grounds bears the unmistakable imprint of Charles Bridgeman, and provide a suitable setting for the house.

ICKWORTH, Suffolk

The Hervey (pronounced Harvey) family has lived near Horringer since the sixteenth century but it was only in 1714 that they came into prominence when John Hervey was created the first Earl of Bristol. His son, another John, became famous for his memoirs of the Court of George II and Molly Lepel, his wife, and it was his third son, Frederick Augustus, who was responsible for the majestic pile that is Ickworth.

Born in 1730, Frederick went into the Church after exercising his privilege as a nobleman's son of becoming an MA without sitting the examination. Similar preferment in later years enabled him to become Bishop of Londonderry in Ireland in 1768. He busied himself about his large and lucrative diocese with an ecumenical zeal and generosity that led to an obelisk being erected in his memory at Ickworth by the people of Derry.

Frederick built on a lavish scale. Downhill, on the headlands of North Derry, and Ballyscullion on the shore of Lough Beg, were palaces that now lie in ruins. Ickworth, his last major project, remains, although he did not live to see the house completed. He died in his beloved Italy in 1803 and the house was not ready for occupation until 1830. 'Capability' Brown chose the site; the round house on Belle Isle on Windermere in Cumbria inspired the elliptical design, and the Sandys brothers, architects for Ballyscullion, were commissioned to build in 1796.

For the last ten years of his roving life the Earl Bishop steadily purchased works of art in Italy with Ickworth in mind. Nearly all these were confiscated by Napoleon's troops in 1798. The present collection of paintings, furniture, and Georgian silver, however, satisfies the most discerning visitor; items collected by the Herveys who were fortunate in having Gainsborough as their local portrait-painter.

The 100-foot-high oval rotunda is linked to two wings, one of which, the east, remains the home of the seventh Marquess. The west is but an empty shell, containing huge corn-bins and a squash court. The park, open all the year, has an enclosure for deer, delightful walks through ancient woodland, and beside the eighteenth-century Canal there is an adventure playground for children. Horse and sheepdog trials are held every autumn.

Below: Self-portrait of Elisabeth Vigée Lebrun
Bottom: The rotunda and orangery

ISLAND HALL, Cambridgeshire

The Roman town of Godmanchester, defined by the roads that still encircle it, has charters dating back to 1214 and it is not surprising, therefore, to find here several ancient farmhouses and town houses that survive among the old thatched and half-timbered cottages.

One such house is Island Hall, a large red-brick building two and a half storeys high with two lower bay wings. This impressive Hall was built in about 1747 for John Jackson, the Receiver-General for Huntingdon, which lies just across the River Ouse. Its name is taken from the island that forms part of the original pleasure-gardens to the house.

The ancestors of the present owners of the house, the Vane Percys, acquired the estate in 1804 to complement the land held from the beginning of the eighteenth century in the parish of Godmanchester and Hemingford Grey, farther down the Ouse. Upheaval came when the RAF requisitioned the hall in the Second World War and for the next thirty years all was neglect. But now the house is restored as its builder might have known it and used as a comfortable family home. The main rooms are panelled in fine Georgian style and contain many interesting items that relate to the family that acquired them.

The gardens in their tranquil riverside setting are open and teas are served.

KENTWELL HALL, Suffolk

This moated Elizabethan mansion, completed in 1563, is anything but a stately home. It was rescued from mouldering oblivion in 1971 by a young lawyer who, since his marriage in 1973, has courageously restored this red-brick house to a state which allows many thousands to enjoy it each year.

Approached by a three-quarters-of-a-mile-long avenue of limes planted in 1678, Kentwell is now familiar to many schoolchildren from all over East Anglia, who return here each summer to re-create the everyday domestic life of the Tudor period. The costumes, the music, the food, the crafts – even the speech – are faithful re-creations. This imaginative approach to education is echoed by the restoration work which is continually in progress in the Hall.

The exterior has altered little since the end of the sixteenth century but inside there has been greater change. The west wing retains many Elizabethan features, such as the fireplaces, panelling, and brickwork; the east and centre wings were substantially remodelled by Thomas Hopper after a fire in 1826.

Outside the south-west corner of the Hall is the half-timbered Moat House where the upstairs room or 'solar' is painted to re-create the décor of the late fifteenth century by using simple earth colours applied to lime plaster.

Black swans glide majestically round the moats that have been dredged and in the paddocks beyond rare breeds of sheep now graze. The outbuildings that await their turn for painstaking restoration reflect the activities and pursuits of the Tudor gentry and their small army of retainers.

There is the vinery, the dovecot – complete with its potence for gathering the young birds – the dog kennels, the pavilion, and the tennis-court lawn. The spacious walled garden has been replanned, the Yew Walk re-created, and the lawns trimmed.

In 1985 the front courtyard was transformed into a brick-paved mosaic maze. The design, created by 25,000 bricks in four hues, presents a perfect Tudor rose some seventy foot across. Images are created within fifteen diamond-shaped plaques and take the form of a signature, an heraldic device, and a symbol representing each Tudor monarch.

LAVENHAM GUILDHALL, Suffolk

No matter where you wander in this remarkably preserved village there are timber-framed buildings to admire, many dating from medieval times when the woollen cloth trade flourished. All paths lead to the Market Place, fronting which is the Guildhall, built in 1528–29 by the Guild of Corpus Christi, one of the four guilds in the village whose functions were social and religious rather than for regulating trade. The guild was suppressed at the time of the Dissolution by Henry VIII and the Guildhall has since only been used for secular purposes – as a prison, a house of correction, a workhouse, an almshouse, a wool store, and even simple housing for evacuees in the Second World War.

It was saved from complete destruction by a Suffolk family and handed over to the National Trust in 1951. Today it houses a local museum with a special display to interpret the woollen cloth industry that reached its zenith in the fifteenth century. There is a working loom, occasionally demonstrated, the like of which would have been found in most Lavenham houses.

Of interest to American visitors is a room dedicated to the memory of the US airmen who flew their wartime missions from many bases round here.

Adjoining the Guildhall is the Old Chapel whose original windows, once unglazed, are now reopened. This medieval room is now used as a tea-room and, upstairs behind the gallery, an information centre. The whole building remains as a centre for the local community with many meetings being held in the thirty-two-foot-long Main Hall, whose doorways, with Tudor arches and carved spandrels, lead to the cellars beneath where are displayed the tools once used by the coopers for making their wooden barrels.

On the east side of the Market Place is Little Hall, built about 1450 for a rich clothier, and now the headquarters of the Suffolk Preservation Society. The soot-blackened crown-post roof of the original hall is of great interest, as is an eclectic collection of furniture, pictures, sculptures, and ceramics that adorns the rooms.

Above: Little Hall
Below: The Guildhall

LAYER MARNEY TOWER, Essex

One of the glories of Essex is this magnificent gatehouse, rising eighty feet from the ground, and from its top giving unrivalled views towards the coast.

Four towers make up the gatehouse, the outer with eight storeys each and the inner with seven. The towers are surmounted by superb Italianate terracotta parapets which, in the early sixteenth century, were an exciting architectural innovation. There is also much elaborate terracotta work round the windows.

Part way up the tower an octagonal room is devoted to an imaginative display about the several families which have lived here, and many are the signals reputed to have been flashed from the tower to the smugglers in the estuary waiting to land their contraband.

The Marney family probably came over with William the Conqueror and it was William Marney who obtained a licence to empark the forest here in 1266. It was not until 1523 in the reign of Henry VIII that Lord Henry Marney decided to erect a grand hall in keeping with the family's position. However both he and his son were dead by 1525, and the building work had to stop and thus the gatehouse dominates the humbler range of buildings that now flank it.

To the south of the house is a long building, also of the sixteenth century, that once housed up to thirty horses and their grooms. The timbered roof is of special interest with pincer-shaped beams. Today there is one long gallery that is used for all manner of functions.

The garden reflects the care which the present owners, the Charringtons, give to all the restoration work here and the griffins in their coat of arms are reproduced in Portland stone atop the brick gateposts.

The Church of St Mary the Virgin is contemporary with the gatehouse and contains the tombs of several Marneys including Lord Henry who had the church built. It was also he who gave to it the iron-bound chest which is at least 500 years old: the wall-painting of St Christopher is just as old.

Grace, daughter of Lord Henry Marney, married Sir Edmund Bedingfeld whose father had built, at Oxburgh in west Norfolk, a moated mansion with a similar eighty-foot-high gatehouse which also remains excellently preserved and in National Trust care.

MANNINGTON HALL, Norfolk

Embattled and moated, Mannington presents a wonderful picture comprised of flint, brick, stone, water – and an elaborate garden that is the main reason for visiting this secluded corner of Norfolk. The Hall, built during the Wars of the Roses in 1460, has seen only three families in its long history. In about 1740 it was bought by Horatio Walpole who was then building Wolterton Hall near by. Another branch of the family had built Houghton Hall in west Norfolk in 1735.

A later Horatio Walpole was eccentric in not only rejecting the grandeur of Wolterton but also in his attitude towards animals, a fondness for which far outweighed that for the fairer sex. The graves of his carriage horses and his racing whippet can still be seen; inside the Hall are Latin texts distinctly uncomplimentary to womankind. He travelled widely and collected some of the interesting garden follies outside, and an arresting marble sculpture of the Madonna and Child for the drawing-room. For students of rural history there are two fascinating estate maps, one of 1565 and another of 1742.

The year 1984 saw the opening of the old walled kitchen garden which is now divided into historic periods with gardens of appropriate design and content including roses known to have been in cultivation at the time. 'When are the roses at their best?' is a question constantly heard, to which the reply must be 'throughout the summer', for with over 1,000 varieties to choose from there is always some colour. At the end of June a Rose Festival is the year's highlight.

There are twenty acres of parkland in which to wander and a waymarked nature trail follows a circular route. A ruined Saxon church and some bizarre Victorian follies are added attractions.

Below: An Edwardian rose, *Gruss an Aachen*, 1909
Bottom: The south and garden front

MELFORD HALL, Suffolk

How fortunate is the large village of Long Melford to have two fine Tudor mansions within a mile of each other. Kentwell lies to the west of the main road to Bury St Edmunds; Melford Hall to the east, a U-shaped sixteenth-century house that may well have been built by the last Abbot of Bury before the Reformation.

The strange, isolated building on Melford Green, called the 'Conduit', once had much to do with the supply of water to the hall beside which two medieval fish-ponds remain, one for coarse fish and the other for trout. Entrance to the hall is under an archway and past an elegant octagonal pavilion once used as an orangery whose faces are crowned with pointed gables and finials.

The lawns, punctuated by hedges of box and yew, lie within the ancient moat, now dry, and some well-grown trees including several rare species provide a superb setting for the warm-red hall whose bricks were fashioned from clay dug from the pond on the green. Beyond the gardens to the north and west the National Trust, the owner, has replanted the avenues of oaks whose lines are clearly shown on an estate map of 1613 now hanging in the Hall.

The first owner of Melford was William Cordell – still a farming name in Suffolk – an astute lawyer who became Speaker of the House of Commons and entertained Queen Elizabeth I here in 1578 together with 2,000 of her retainers. A fine portrait of the Queen in stained glass is in a window of the east gallery.

The property changed hands several times and then in 1786 Sir Harry Parker, related to the Parkers of Saltram House at Plymouth (another Trust property) bought the Hall, and his descendant, Sir Richard Hyde Parker, now lives here. Sir Harry's father, brother, and nephew all became distinguished Admirals whose portraits can be seen in the Hall together with the sea charts they used and paintings of their famous sea engagements.

The maritime flavour is strengthened by the superb collection of Chinese famille rose and verte porcelain taken from a captured Spanish galleon in 1762 that was bearing gifts from the Emperor of Peking to the King of Spain.

Two upstairs rooms are a reminder that the children's writer, Beatrix Potter, often came to stay at Melford. She was a first cousin of the Hyde Parkers and 'tried out' several of her stories on their children. A Melford fireplace appears in *The Tailor of Gloucester* and a stuffed model of Jemima Puddleduck that Beatrix Potter used for her paintings can be seen beside some of her original work.

Below: The bedroom used by Beatrix Potter
Bottom: The Library

OXBURGH HALL, Norfolk

Once surrounded by marsh and heath Oxburgh remains hard to find but diligence is rewarded by the first view of this moated, fortified manor house, home to the Bedingfeld family for over 500 years. Sir Edmund obtained a licence from Edward IV in 1482 to build walls, towers, and battlements and the Charter, complete with massive seal, is in the Hall today. His direct descendant, Henry, now lives in the south-west tower and it was his grandmother who saw that the National Trust took over the Hall in 1952.

The family has always supported the Catholic and Royalist causes and suffered – or prospered – accordingly. In the mighty gate-tower the visitor can enter, with difficulty, a cunning hiding hole constructed for priests about 1578. In 1497 King Henry VII and his Queen, Elizabeth of York, accompanied by their courtiers spent two nights here and used the same circular brick staircase that links all the rooms in the gate-tower. In the room used by the Queen there now hangs an elaborate tapestry map of 1647 depicting all the towns and villages in Oxfordshire and surrounding counties. In the King's room is a fine portrait of Sir Henry, Governor of the Tower of London when Elizabeth was incarcerated there.

Another Royal connection are the superb green velvet embroidered panels that hang in one of the rooms in dim splendour so as to preserve their delicate shades. These are the work of Mary Queen of Scots, and Elizabeth, Countess of Shrewsbury, in about 1569.

The variety of architectural styles at Oxburgh can best be appreciated by clambering up on to the roof of the gate-tower to admire the Gothic Revival chimneys and battlements, and beyond to the walled garden. Apart from the tower the rooms inside are decorated in the Victorian style of Pugin and Buckler but contain family portraits and furniture that span the centuries. The chapel in the grounds contains, behind the altar, a remarkable Bruges triptych.

Below: The spiral staircase in the gate-tower
Bottom: The gate-tower and north face reflected in the wide moat

PECKOVER HOUSE, Cambridgeshire

Wisbech justly claims to be the 'Capital of the Fens', a port on the River Nene which today flows another ten miles before reaching the sea. But in the eighteenth century a large fleet of coasters was based here with cargo being transhipped for the trade to the interior. Wealthy merchants built their elegant houses along both 'Brinks' or banks of the river, after the Dutch style, and Peckover House is perhaps the finest surviving example, dating from 1722.

The name is an uncommon one, adapted from Pickenhaver, and the founder of this powerful Wisbech family was a soldier in Cromwell's army during the Civil War. He became a Quaker and his son Jonathan bought Bank House as it was called in 1777. He went into partnership with the Gurneys of Norwich, established a bank in the south wing and it was his grandson who finally merged the banking interests with others to form Barclays Bank in 1896. At one time 'Peckover' banknotes were preferred to those of the Bank of England.

The classic exteriors of the house – the garden front is the more impressive – give no hint of the elaborate decoration within. The rooms are panelled, the fireplaces have intricate carved overmantels, and moulded plasterwork shows how well the craftsmen in Georgian times could perform. None of the furniture in the house belonged to the Peckovers, except one firescreen embroidered by a daughter of the house that turned up at auction and was bought by the Trust.

In the library there now hangs a collection of martial portraits of the Cornwallis family and in a room at the head of the original 1722 staircase is displayed a small exhibition about Octavia Hill, the Victorian philanthropist who was born in a house opposite on the South Brink. She helped to found the National Trust in 1895 and was a great friend of the Peckovers.

For most the chief glory of Peckover is the twelve-acre Victorian garden complete with summer-houses, ponds, colourful herbaceous borders, shrubberies, and serpentine, grassy paths. In the traditional greenhouse are three orange trees that, even after 250 years, continue to fruit and round them the dedicated gardener arranges pots of exotic plants. The maidenhair tree (ginkgo) growing here was the tallest in the land until 'topped' by a recent gale.

Below: The drawing room
Bottom: The garden front

SANDRINGHAM HOUSE, Norfolk

As their son 'Bertie' approached his twenty-first birthday his parents, Queen Victoria and her consort, Albert, searched for an estate which would be a healthy country retreat for him, as Osborne and Balmoral were to them. Even Albert's death from typhoid could not delay this project and Sandringham was bought in 1862 some two months after his decease. A direct rail link had been in operation since 1847, and the shooting in these parts was – and remains – excellent. Within a few months the Prince of Wales married Princess Alexandra. Georgian Sandringham, despite many additions, proved too small and so the main block was demolished and a new house, in the Jacobean style, replaced it. The old conservatory remained to become the billiard room. A bowling-alley was added in the same style and – to cater for the Prince of Wales's maturing taste – a ballroom was added later still. Queen Victoria was more than amused; she found the new house 'handsome' and duly planted an oak to mark her approbation, so starting a passion for planting specimen trees which our Royal Family has indulged ever since.

At the same time the grounds were replanned. An ill-placed lake near the house was filled in while two new lakes were excavated. The result is a water landscape that follows the traditions of great landscape-designers such as 'Capability' Brown. Fringed with rockeries, colourful shrubs and trees both exotic and native, the lakes are perfect mirrors for the house.

But the grounds are by no means of one period in style. To the north of the house stands a magnificent avenue of pleached limes, harking back to Shakespeare's day. The formality of the crenellated hedge to the north-east contrasts with the flower gardens, where colour runs riot in the many and various flower-beds. Equally eye-catching are the areas devoted to camellias, azaleas, and rhododendrons; to heathers, hydrangeas and polyanthus. From spring to late summer the beautifully tended gardens are a pleasure to walk through. For tree-lovers, the grounds are a happy hunting ground with many unusual specimens. Outside the grounds, the Sandringham Country Park offers a nature trail, walks of differing lengths, a picnic area, and another for interpretation. Of perhaps as much interest as the House is the Church of St Mary Magdalene which is resplendent with gifts from royalty and other distinguished visitors. The altar and reredos are of solid silver and the oak pulpit is covered in the same metal. The nearby disused Wolferton railway station has been made into an intriguing museum of royal railway travel.

Left: Her Majesty the Queen in the drawing-room
Below: Queen Victoria, 1845, by Winterhalter
Bottom: The Saloon, showing the Minstrels' Gallery

SOMERLEYTON HALL, Suffolk

Somerleyton spells exuberance. Some country houses are refined, some are grandiose, others are historical, but Somerleyton and its grounds convey a sense of enjoyment: even its architecture contributes to this feeling. The present house is Victorian. Its wealthy (and later bankrupt) railway-building creator spared no expense to bring stone from France to blend with red brick into a house which seems to be in an English style of some 300 years ago but with strong overtones of Italian influence. The three-storeyed porch on the western front is Jacobean in feeling but the forceful dormer windows and the campanile are imports from the Mediterranean.

The present house enclosed the genuinely Jacobean house built some seven years after the first Queen Elizabeth's death. As can be seen from pictures – and a doll's house modelled on them – this house had most beautifully curved gables; an early indication of the sense of fun which is so strong here but which was probably not apparent to Colonel Oliver Cromwell, when he sacked the house in 1642.

One very Victorian trait, not always over-popular with succeeding generations, was to decorate rooms in a gigantic style. Until 1920 Somerleyton possessed a banqueting hall with a twenty-foot-high fireplace, which ended eight feet short of the ceiling. A sensible alteration about 1920 divided this room into two storeys.

The oak parlour, darkly panelled and richly tapestried, represents the previous house; the dining-room, in the 'Adam style', a later development of it. The library, with light oak bookshelves and fireplace offset by a splendid Savonnerie carpet, is now a living-room and the drawing-room's crimson, gold, and white decoration makes a ballroom fit for a king.

The Royal Palace of Hampton Court has a maze; so has Somerleyton. While planted only one and a quarter centuries ago, the idea of the maze comes from antiquity. No Minotaur, nor strange beast lurk at the centre of this maze, but there are some unusual animals to be seen in the Children's Farm which occupies part of the walled garden. Near by there is an aviary and a miniature railway. All (but the last in particular), although modern innovations, would surely meet with the whole-hearted approval of Somerleyton's Victorian entrepreneur just as they please today's visiting families.

The gardens, beautifully kept, have changed little since Victorian times and are complemented by greenhouses which contain a fine display of hot-house plants.

Left: The maze
Below: The garden front

ST OSYTH'S PRIORY, Essex

Being near a coastal creek made it all too easy for the Danish Vikings in AD 653 to destroy the nunnery established here by Ositha, daughter of the first Christian King of East Anglia. She herself suffered martyrdom, became a Saint, and the site continued in monastic use until Henry VIII dissolved the abbey in 1539.

Only fragments of the original abbey or priory buildings remain but their former splendour can be easily gauged by gazing at the existing gatehouse that was built in about 1475 and recently restored. The outer face is decorated with an elaborate tracery of white stone set in black, knapped flints, and the interior of the archway displays delicate fan vaulting. The low range of buildings either side of it are where the present owners of the Priory live and in the east-wing rooms there can occasionally be viewed a fascinating miscellany of furniture and pictures. In one room is a 1390 fresco of a medieval maiden; in another a highly decorated Victorian WC pedestal, now regarded as a work of art.

Climb to the top of the Abbots Tower erected by Lord d'Arcy in 1558 as part of a range of domestic buildings, now demolished, and see laid out below the lawns and secretive gardens within well-tended shrubs and hedges. The rose-garden represents the geometrical fashion favoured by the Tudors and Stuarts; next to it are the carefully clipped evergreens of the topiary garden.

Deer and peacocks roam in the park, a peaceful atmosphere pervades the whole site with its mixture of architectural styles wrought by medieval, Tudor and Georgian craftsmen. The mid-sixteenth-century tithe barn west of the gatehouse has a roof supported by an intricate tracery of beams and in the Church of SS Peter and Paul the brick-built piers and arches display a mastery of the mason's art. The D'Arcys (the family who owned the Priory from the Dissolution until late in the last century), are commemorated in wall monuments.

Below: Drawing-room of the Georgian wing, showing the life-size painting of 'Whistle-Jacket', by George Stubbs
Bottom: The fifteenth-century gatehouse

WIMPOLE HALL, Cambridgeshire

Sited as it is on the boundary of Cambridgeshire and Hertfordshire, Wimpole is important for not only being the largest country house in the former county but for possessing a landscape of rare historical worth. There are no less than three medieval villages whose skeletons of ditch, boundary, and pathway can be traced in the turf of Wimpole's 350-acre park. Between the warren that once teemed with rabbits and the west wing of the Hall is an undulating area, ribbed with the ridges and furrows used for medieval crops of corn and roots.

From 1640, when Thomas Chichely built an 'extraordinary, curious neat house' on the site of an ancient, moated manor house, until the 1950s, the Hall and park surrounding it have experienced constant change at the hands of landscape and building architects alike. Henry Flitcroft, Gibbs, John Soane, and finally Kendall, were all commissioned to alter and embellish the house while Kent, Bridgeman, Brown and Repton – whose Red Book can be seen in the Hall – strove to improve on nature by planting avenues and clumps of trees, digging lakes and raising a ruinous folly.

An engraving by Kip dated 1707 shows a landscape of contrived extravagance that finally made Wimpole's second owner, Lord Radnor, bankrupt. A similar fate befell the third owner, Edward Harley, second Earl of Oxford, whose passion for collecting manuscripts and paintings forced him to sell Wimpole in 1740. But at least he had the satisfaction of knowing that his collection was the foundation of the first British Library. The Yorke family then bought the estate and were to remain owners until the fifth Earl of Hardwicke, immortalised in the music-hall song 'Champagne Charlie', squandered his fortune and was forced to sell in 1894.

Wimpole, almost emptied of its contents, was finally saved by Captain George Bambridge and his wife, Elsie, who had access to the royalties earned by her father, Rudyard Kipling. She demolished the Victorian wings with their towers, restored the rooms to something like their original elegance, and then bequeathed the estate to the National Trust on her death in 1976.

Today the visitor can admire the perfect symmetry of Gibbs's double-cube library; the painted interior of the Chapel; and the domed yellow drawing-room by John Soane who also designed a bath-house for the gouty Georgian owners of Wimpole.

The south avenue, double-planted by Bridgeman with elms in 1721, is now replanted with limes and all two and a half miles is back in Trust ownership.

There is access to the woodland and park by waymarked paths. The bridges are rebuilt and even the commanding ruins made safe. The restored Kendall stable block once more rings to the sound of the hooves of heavy horses – Suffolk Punches – and doubles as a reception point for visitors to this historic and lively estate.

Below: Lord Chancellor Somers, father-in-law of the first Earl of Hardwicke
Bottom: The south front

WIMPOLE HOME FARM, Cambridgeshire

While on the Grand Tour of Europe in 1779 the third Earl of Hardwicke met the gifted architect John Soane and promised him on his return a chance to design something new and exciting at Wimpole. The result was not only an elegant set of rooms for the Hall but a model farm for the park. Built of tarred timber walls on brick footings and roofs of thatch and slate, the farm buildings survived nearly intact but dilapidated until 1976 when the National Trust took over the estate.

It was only a timely search through the drawings in the Soane Museum in London that saved the buildings from demolition as their Soane provenance had not been suspected. Now restored with traditional reed thatch, the Home Farm range of sheds and the 180-foot-long Great Barn are the home and shelter for a wide range of endangered breeds of domestic animals. In this approved rare-breeds centre are three types of cattle, goats, sheep, poultry, pigs and even draughthorses.

The animals graze on the 350 acres of pasture in the park and the roan-red longhorn cattle are in perfect keeping with the Hall commanding the background. The more docile breeds are to be found in the Children's Corner where lambs appear to gambol throughout the season. There is also an adventure playground. The dairy has been restored to its Victorian splendour with gleaming coloured tiles; the Great Barn houses a collection of over 650 implements the like of which were used on the farm during the last 150 years, and in a loft films about Wimpole and farming in general are projected continuously.

A farm trail begins and ends at the Home Farm and takes the visitor round the neighbouring arable farmland which is in striking contrast to the park pastures.

Below: An old hay wain, part of the Home Farm collection
Bottom: The restored Great Barn

WINGFIELD COLLEGE, Suffolk

The neo-classical façade of the college building and the fine Church of St Andrew that overlooks it conceal behind their quiet exteriors many pointers to the turbulent history of England. Sir John de Wingfield, a close friend of the Black Prince, distinguished himself at the Battle of Poitiers and determined to found a College with ransom money wrung from the French. Tragically he was struck down by the Black Death in 1361 and his wife was left to seal the College Charter a year later. The College flourished until it was surrendered to Henry VIII in 1542.

The founder's daughter, Katherine, married the grandson of William atte Pool (to become de la Pole) who had founded the town of Kingston-upon-Hull. Their grandson, William, was created the first Duke of Suffolk and married the granddaughter of Geoffrey Chaucer. His fate was to be beheaded over the gunwale of a boat after being caught while fleeing to France; his end is recounted in Shakespeare's *Henry VI*.

The college itself was built on the site of an existing manor house whose Great Hall was incorporated into the new range of buildings. The construction of the timber framing from oak makes use of ingenious 'scarf' joints that were in use from about 1250 onwards. In the mid eighteenth century, when the college and the church were in a ruinous condition, Squire Buck, in order to keep up with his neighbours, turned the college into a Georgian country house with a superficial Palladian front. Behind this the medieval floors were lowered, ceilings raised and no less than three rooms were built into the Great Hall. For 200 years this drastic rebuilding of Wingfield remained undetected and not until 1971 did the work of restoration begin. The rooms shown to the visitor today are a fascinating portrayal of domestic architecture over five centuries and outside comparison between the east and west elevations further strengthens the belief that here indeed is a story-book of building, written in wood, stone and plaster.

In the north and south chapels of the collegiate church are three fine Wingfield monuments, carved in wood, including one to commemorate the founder. Just to the south is a lovely Georgian farmhouse and, to complete the rural setting, an unspoilt pub.

The college is now the home of a flourishing annual season of arts and music; there are guided tours for parties and schoolchildren, and the topiary and old kitchen gardens provide a worthy setting for such enterprise.

Left: The Great Hall, *c.* 1300
Below: The west Palladian front